I0016182

How a Hard Drive Works.

Camboard Publishing

Camboard Publishing
Cambridge. Great Britain.

www.camboard-publishing.com

Age range 11+

The hard disk drive is the primary device used for storing data. Every personal computer has a hard drive built into the machine.

How a Hard Drive Works shows with full color illustrations, the main functions and operations of a primary internal hard disk drive.

Reading data from the hard disk is shown with full color illustrations.

The workings of the E-IDE controller are explained.

Writing data to the hard disk is shown with full color illustrations.

The file allocation table, sectors, tracks and clusters are covered in How a Hard Drive Works.

This book will be useful to students and anyone else wishing to learn about How a Hard Drive Works.

How a Hard Drive Works

Contents

Chapter 1

Introduction.

The hard disk drive is the primary device used for storing data.

Every computer has a hard drive built into the machine.

The computer's hard drive is where the operating system, and most installed programs are loaded from.

Hard Drive

Chapter 1. Introduction.

With its high-speed operation programs can be loaded quickly.

When buying a new computer, it's a good idea to buy a machine whose hard drive, has a large storage capacity and fast access time..

Hard Drive

Hard Disk Drive

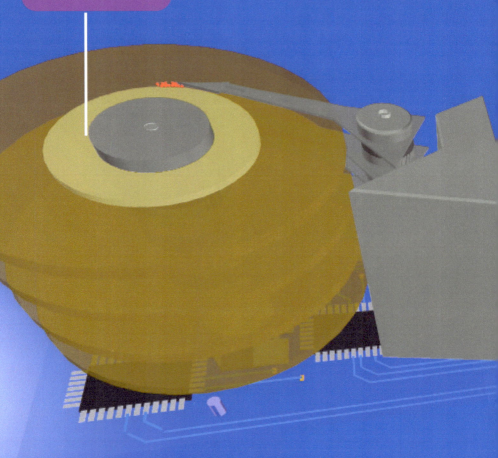

A hard drive can typically store many gigabytes of data, a CD-ROM disk is limited to 650 megabytes.

The access time governs how fast data can be retrieved, from the hard drives disks.

Chapter 1. Introduction.

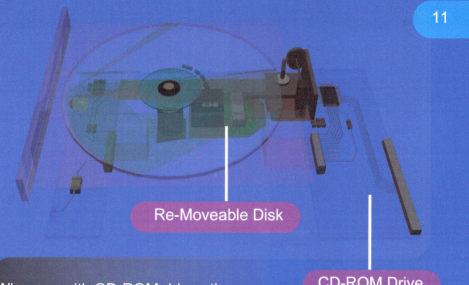

Re-Moveable Disk

CD-ROM Drive

Whereas with CD-ROM drives the storage media is not permanent, with a hard drive the disks are contained in the case.

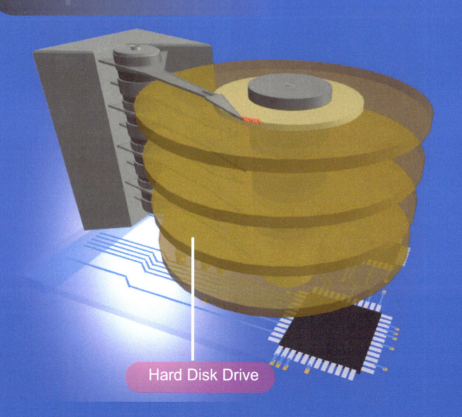

Hard Disk Drive

Hard Disk Drive.

Magnetic Platter

The drive features a number of magnetic revolving platters.

The platters spin at a huge speed, this allows data to be written and retrieved very quickly.

Although data access times are fast, they are not as quick as the computers own system memory.

System Memory

The drive is contained in a sealed case to keep out dust and foreign particles, which would otherwise damage the delicate surface of each platter.

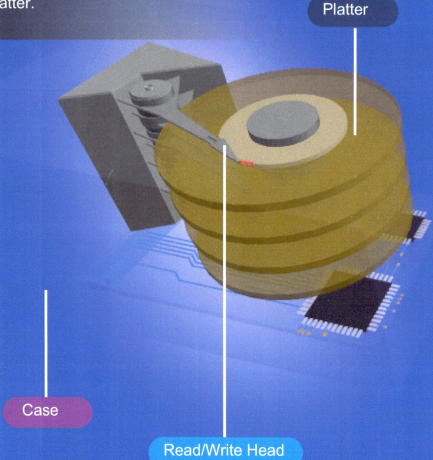

Platter

Case

Read/Write Head

On the platter surface is a thin magnetic coating. Anything trapped between the surface and read/write heads, could damage the coating. The number of platters and coating, composition determine the amount of data the drive will hold.

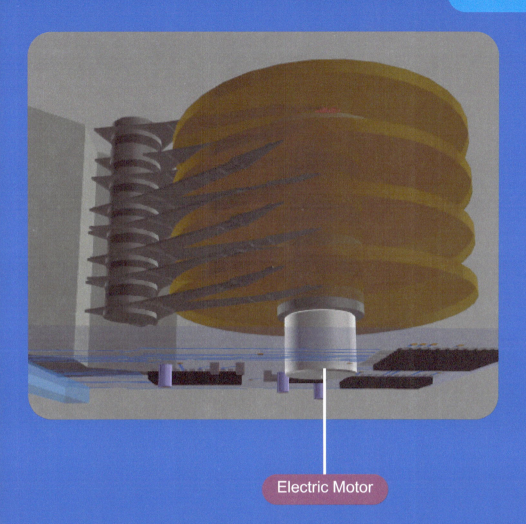

Electric Motor

An electric motor spins the metal or glass platter at speeds of up to 10'000 rpm.

Platters.

Magnetic Surface

The magnetic surface allows data to be written onto it and be stored.

When power is switched off, the data is still held on the platters.

Chapter 1. Introduction.

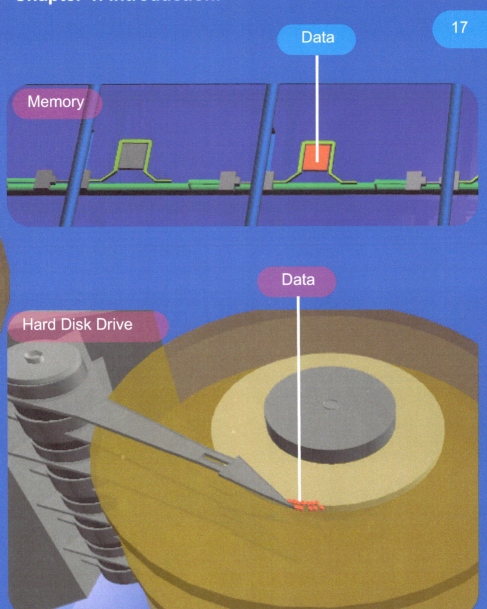

Data

Memory

Data

Hard Disk Drive

Reading and writing data with the disk, is relatively slow compared to memory.

Access times are typically in milliseconds.

Moving Arm

Read/Write Head

Actuator

Chapter 1. Introduction.

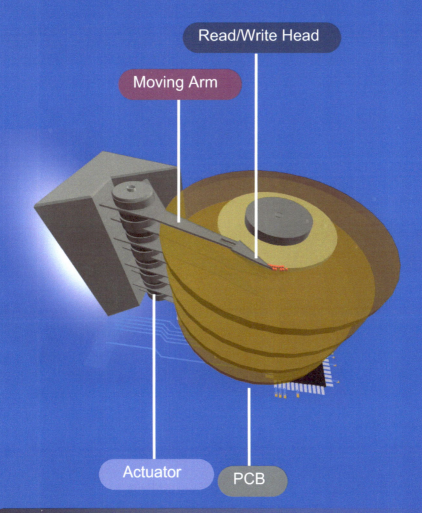

Read/Write Head

Moving Arm

Actuator

PCB

A read/write head is dedicated to each platter, and the head is attached to a moving arm.
An actuator positions the arm in a precise location, across the platter.
The head writes data from the disk controller to the platter, or reads data from the platter.
Underneath the platters is a printed circuit board (PCB), which controls the positions of the read/write heads enabling data to be read or written.

On a E-IDE (Enhanced - Integrated Drive Electronics) hard disk the disk controller, receives commands from the operating system and BIOS.

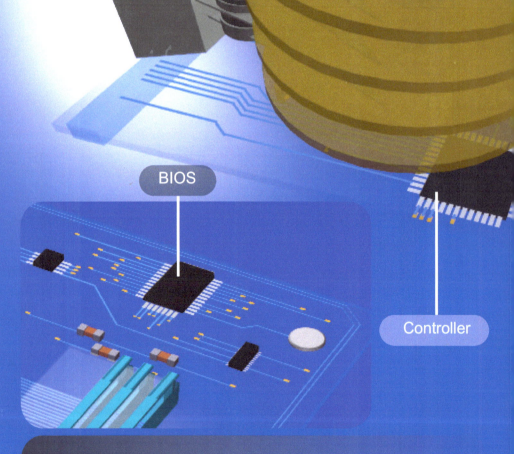

BIOS

Controller

The BIOS is a chip that is on the PC's motherboard. The BIOS contains software code that loads a software driver to enable the hard disk to work.

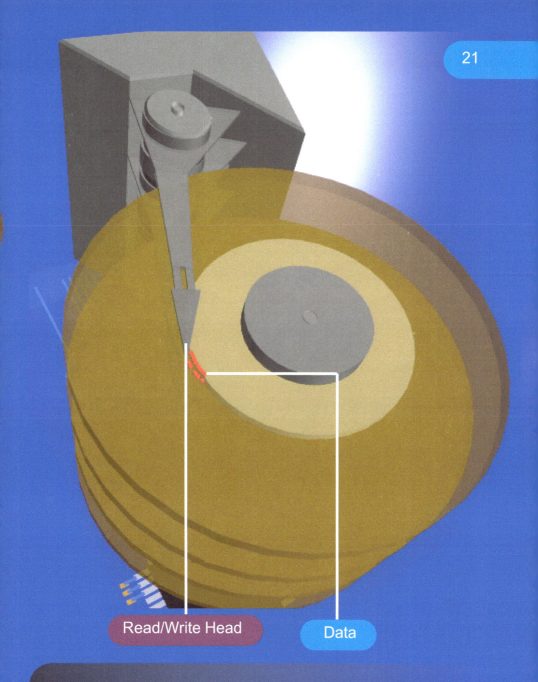

Read/Write Head

Data

The circuitry translates these into positions for the read/write heads to move to, and whether to read in data, or write new data, onto the platter surface.
The circuitry has the job of keeping a constant speed for the drives electric motor.

Read/Write Head

Read/Write heads move across the platter on arms, to read or write data onto the drive.

The arms move at high speed to access data at any given location.

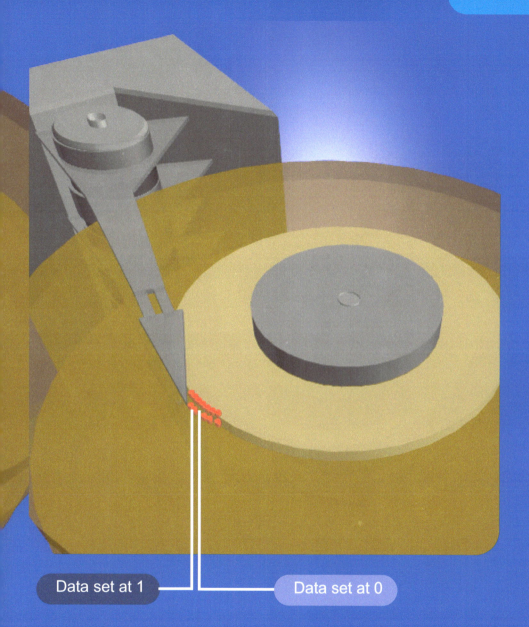

Data set at 1

Data set at 0

Data is stored magnetically as binary 1 or 0.
Existing data can be overwritten by new data.

Chapter 2

E-IDE.

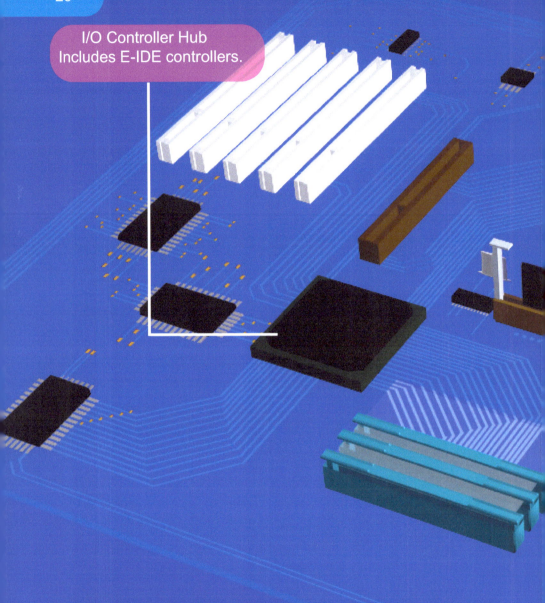

I/O Controller Hub
Includes E-IDE controllers.

Because there are so many different hard disks available, your computer includes an E-IDE (Enhanced-Integrated Drive Electronics) controller, which communicates between the computers system bus and hard drive.

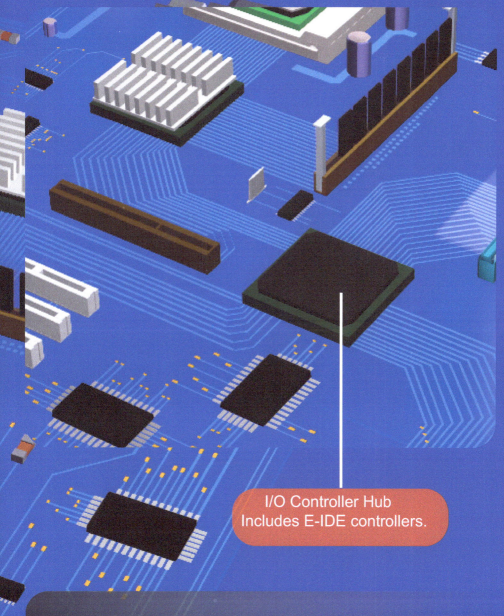

I/O Controller Hub
Includes E-IDE controllers.

This standard ensures hard drives that are compatible with the E-IDE standard, can work with an E-IDE compatible computer. Virtually all PCs come with an E-IDE controller built into the motherboard.

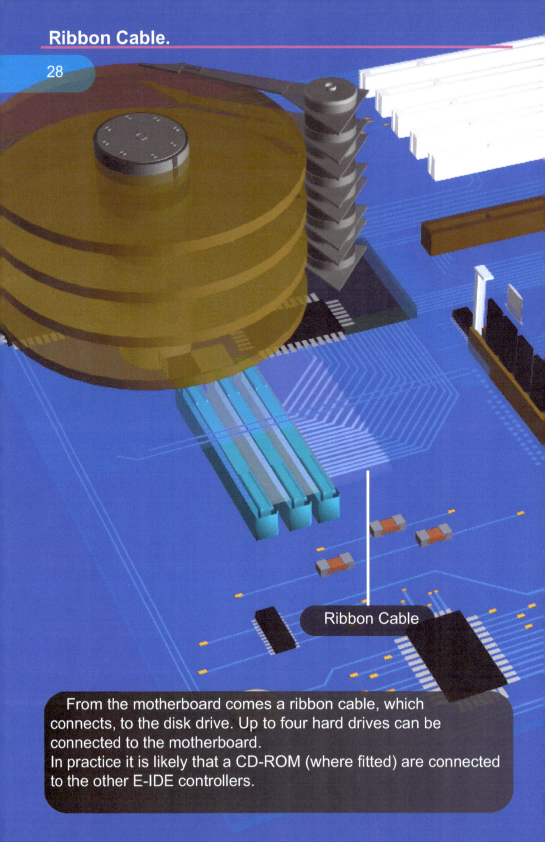

Ribbon Cable

From the motherboard comes a ribbon cable, which connects, to the disk drive. Up to four hard drives can be connected to the motherboard.
In practice it is likely that a CD-ROM (where fitted) are connected to the other E-IDE controllers.

If two hard drives are connected on the same cable, signals are sent to both. One drive is called the master the other a slave. The BIOS tells which drive the data is for, although both drives receive the data, only one uses the data, the other drive ignores it.
The E-IDE controller merely passes the commands and data to the drive in a format it understands.

Master

Slave

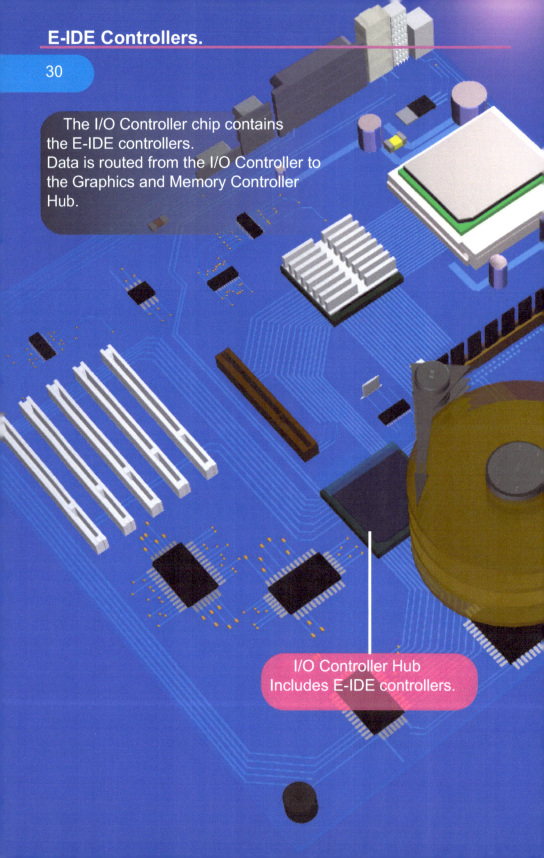

The I/O Controller chip contains the E-IDE controllers.
Data is routed from the I/O Controller to the Graphics and Memory Controller Hub.

I/O Controller Hub
Includes E-IDE controllers.

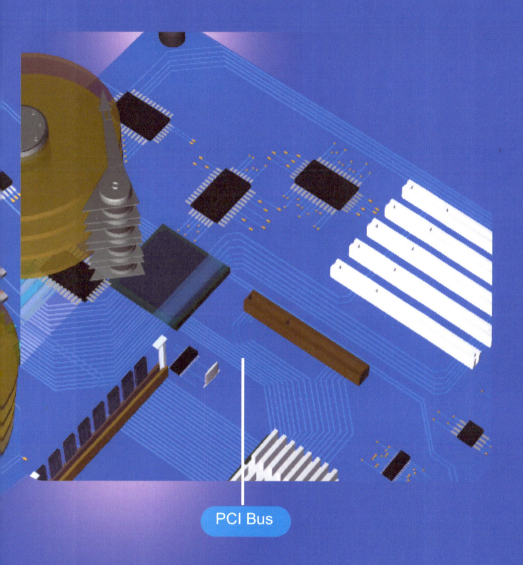

PCI Bus

From here the data is placed onto the PCI bus to the CPU.

Chapter 3

Reading Data.

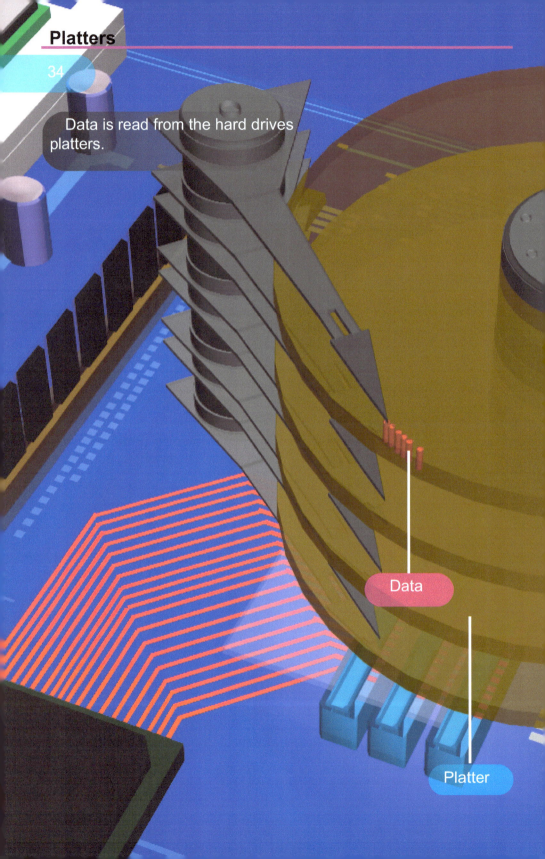

Data is read from the hard drives platters.

Data

Platter

Read/Write head

The Read/Write heads move to where data is and then read this data.

Hard Disk Controller

Data moves from the hard disk drive, into the hard disk controller.

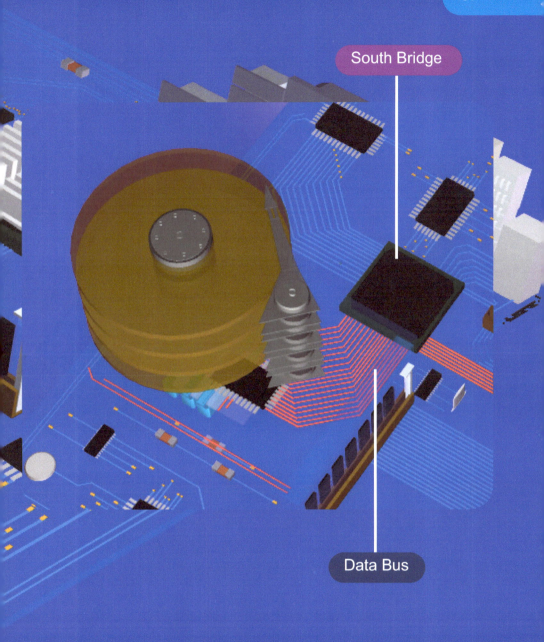

South Bridge

Data Bus

Data is then moved from the hard disk controller to the South Bridge.

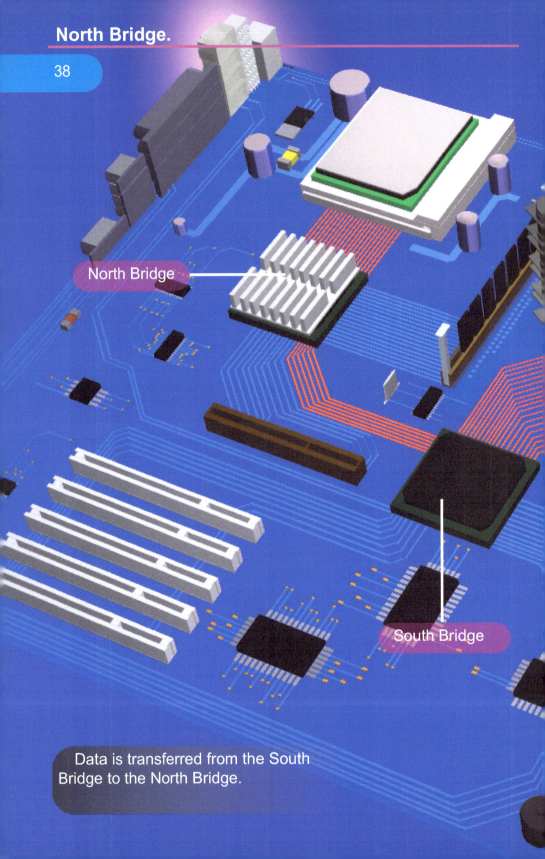

North Bridge

South Bridge

Data is transferred from the South
Bridge to the North Bridge.

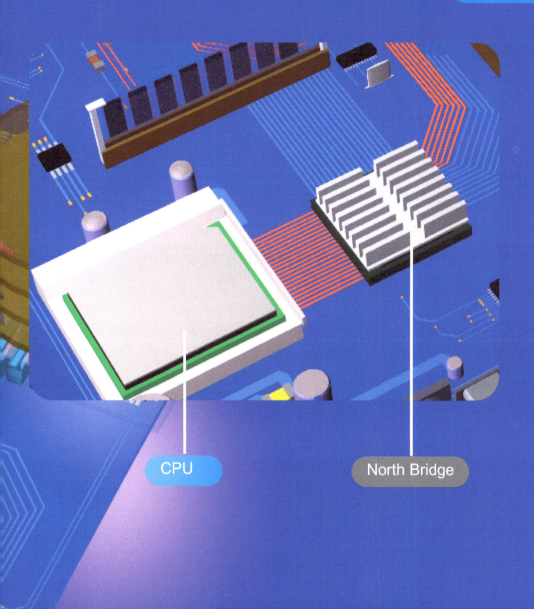

CPU

North Bridge

Data is transferred from the North Bridge to the CPU.

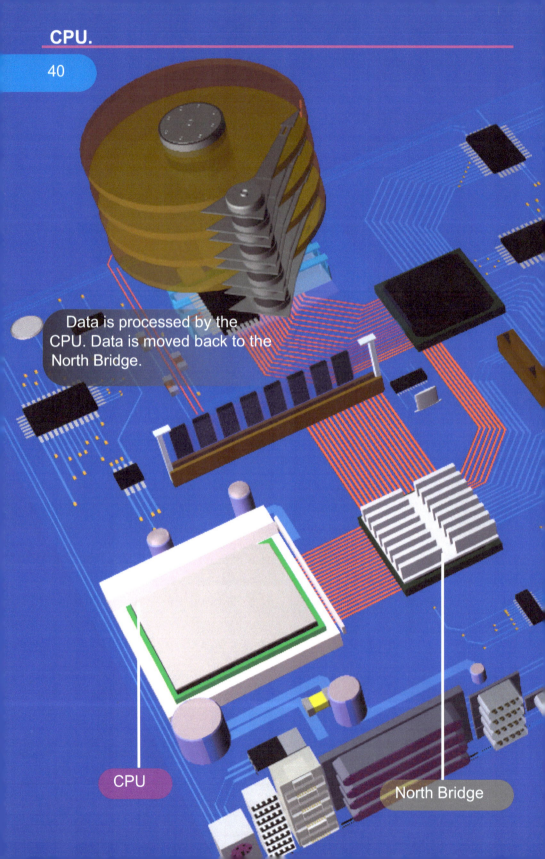

Data is processed by the CPU. Data is moved back to the North Bridge.

CPU

North Bridge

Chapter 3. Reading Data.

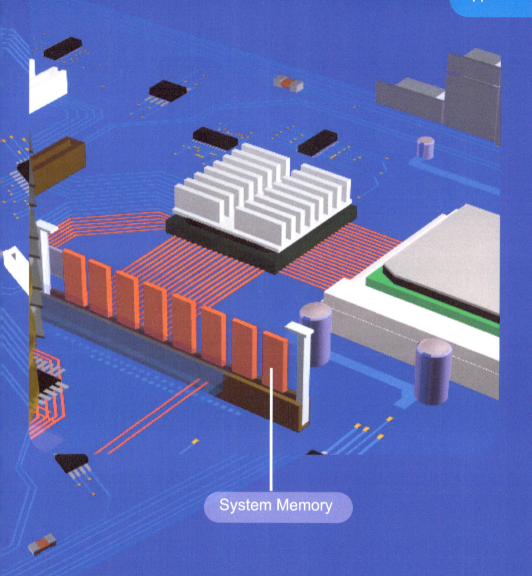

System Memory

Data is processed by the CPU.
Data is moved back to the North
Bridge.
Data is then moved to the main system
memory.

Chapter 4

Writing Data.

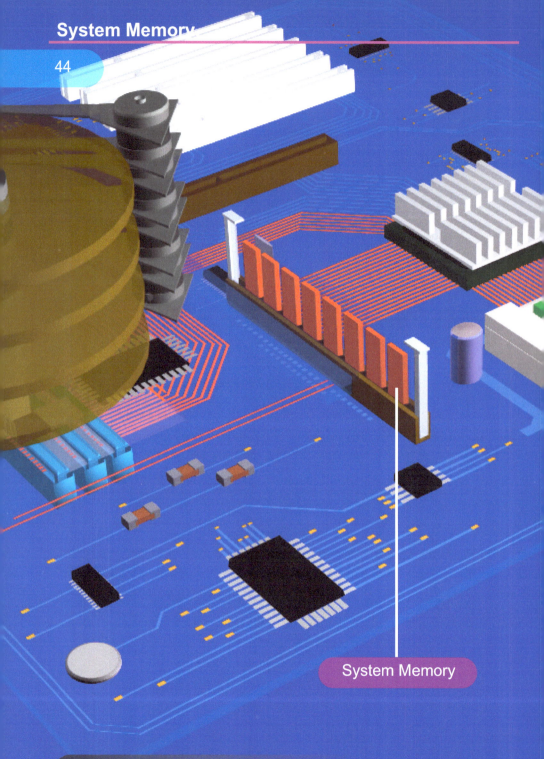

System Memory

Data is retrieved from system memory
and moved to the North Bridge.

Chapter 4. Writing Data.

Data is moved from the North Bridge.
Data is then moved to the CPU.
Data is processed by the CPU.

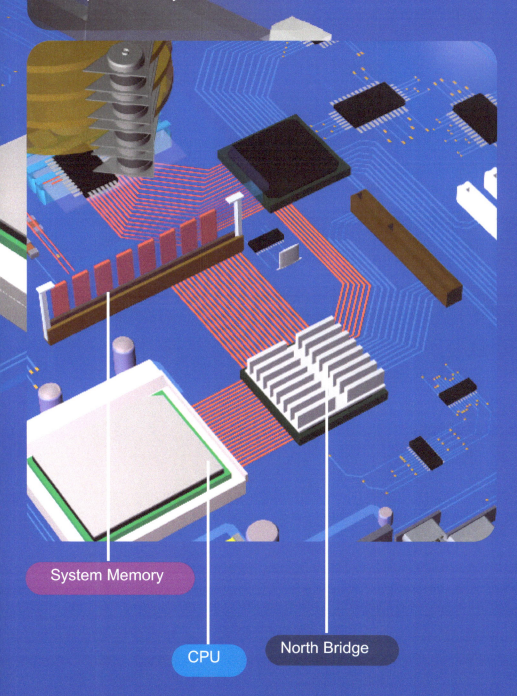

System Memory

CPU

North Bridge

Data is moved from the CPU to North Bridge.

CPU

North Bridge

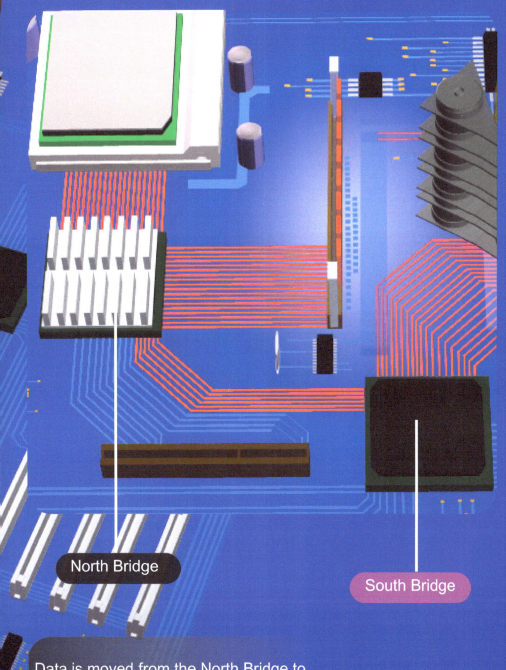

North Bridge

South Bridge

Data is moved from the North Bridge to the South Bridge.

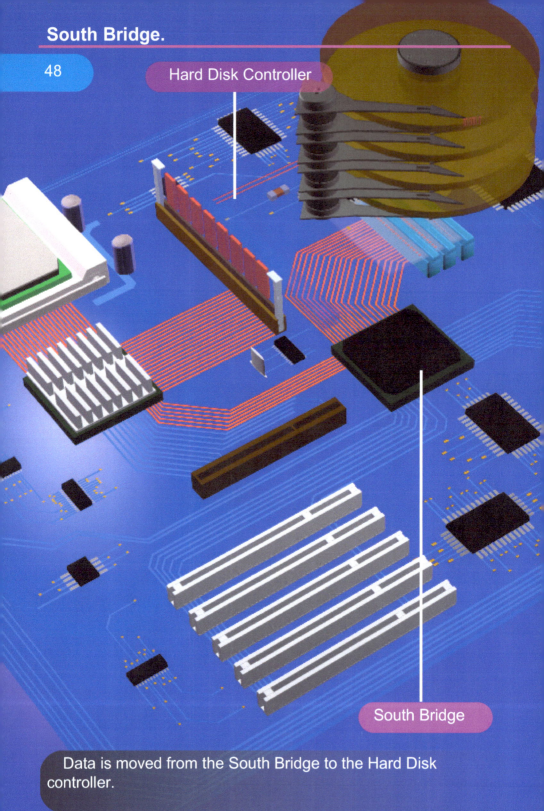

Hard Disk Controller

South Bridge

Data is moved from the South Bridge to the Hard Disk controller.

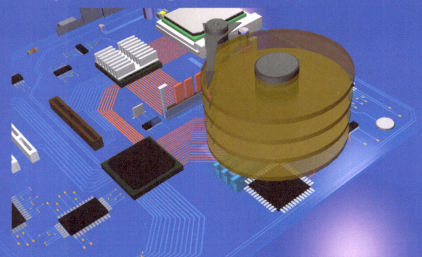

Data is moved from the Hard Disk controller to the hard disk.

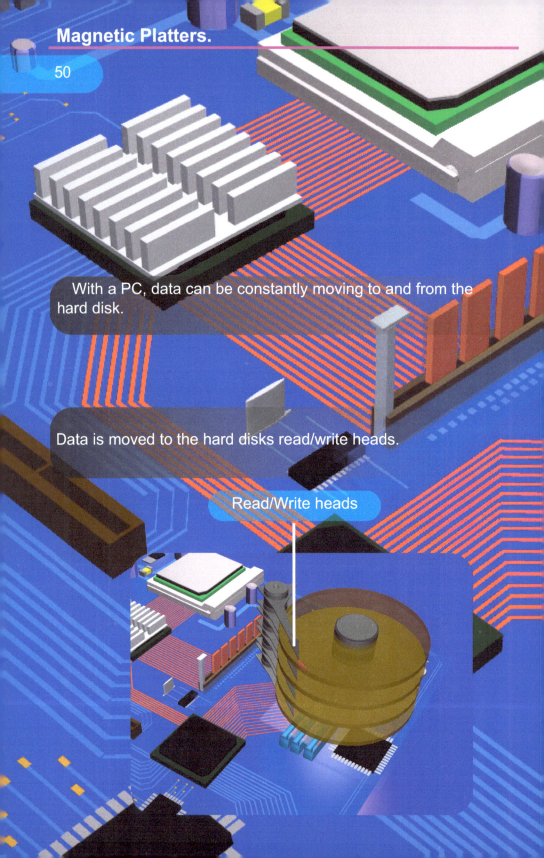

Magnetic Platters.

With a PC, data can be constantly moving to and from the hard disk.

Data is moved to the hard disks read/write heads.

Read/Write heads

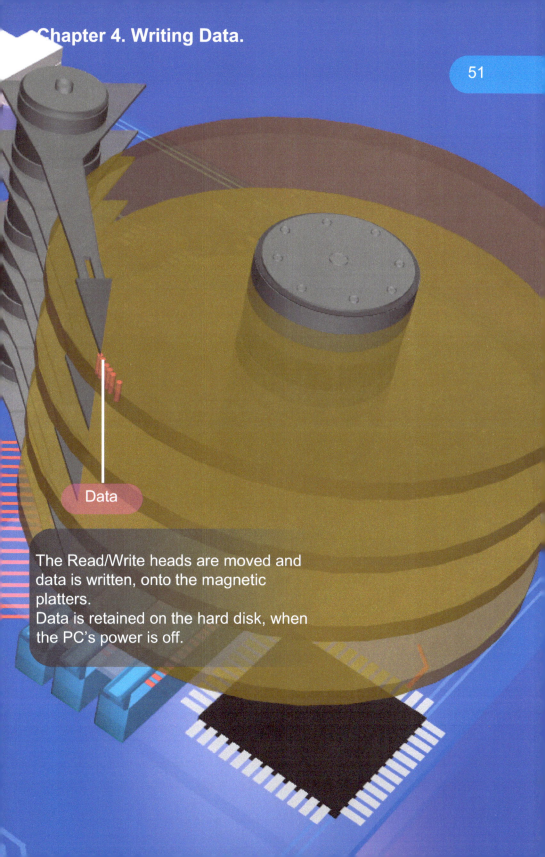

Data

The Read/Write heads are moved and data is written, onto the magnetic platters.
Data is retained on the hard disk, when the PC's power is off.

Chapter 5

File Allocation Table (FAT).

When a file is read or written, the operating system issues a command which orders the hard disk controller, to move the read/write heads to the drives file allocation table (FAT, FAT32, VFAT,NTFS) NTFS is the version used in Windows 10.

FAT

 The operating system reads in the FAT to determine which cluster holds the beginning section of a file. In a write operation which part of the disk is available to hold the file.

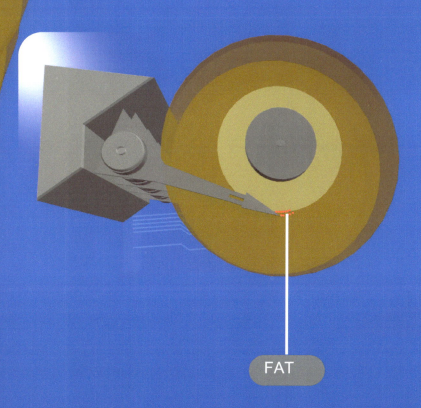

FAT

A file maybe split across many clusters, so the o.s keeps a record of the cluster positions used by a file in the drives file allocation table (FAT).
This file is usually stored in the first cluster(s) which are free on a hard drives platters.
When a file is saved, the FAT is checked by the operating system to find the next unwritten free clusters.

FAT

File stored in separate clusters

When the FAT data has passed through the drives electrics, the operating system instructs the read/write heads to write data to the free clusters.

After this the heads are sent back to the FAT, where it writes to the platter a list of the files clusters.

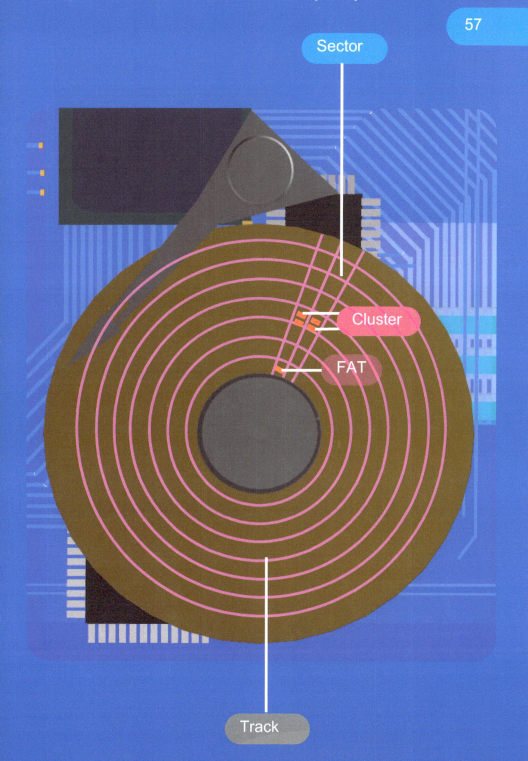

Sector

Cluster

FAT

Track

Before any data can be saved on a hard drive, the disks must be formatted. This is usually done, by the makers of your computer, so you don't need to do it yourself.

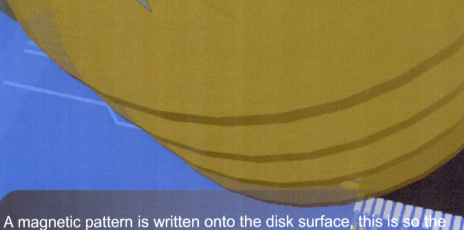

A magnetic pattern is written onto the disk surface, this is so the disk controller can keep track of where the read/write heads are in relation to the disk.

This pattern consists of sectors and tracks. When the read/write heads move across the disk it can read these markers so it can tell where it is.

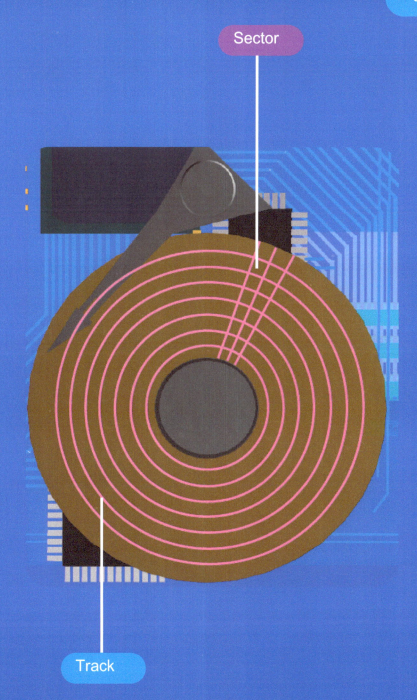

Sector

Track

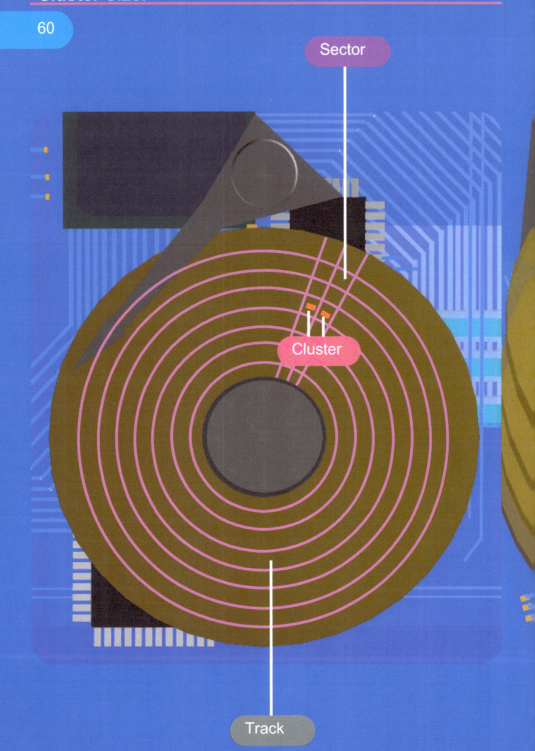

At least two or more sectors on a single track make up a cluster or block. The cluster size varies with the size of disk and operating system used.
The number of clusters that are on the disk's surface, determine the disk size.

For Windows XP or higher using FAT32.

Drive Size	Cluster Size
256MB - 8GB	4KB
8GB – 16GB	8KB
16GB – 32GB	16KB

www.ingramcontent.com/pod-product-compliance
Lightning Source LLC
Chambersburg PA
CBHW041153050326
40690CB00001B/456